AF446622

BROKEN HEARTED

I Have Been Damaged By A Woman Who Has Been Torn Apart By So Many Men, She Infiltrated Me Through Sharing Warm And Pleasing Dialogue; She Cling 2 Me 4 Her On Purpose Cause When She Needed Love She Came Straight Towards My Way 4 It, So Dexterous How Could A Man Not Fall 4 Her; So In Love With Her Physical And Mental Attraction I Was Blinded Right Along With The Love Making Passion, Sleeping In My Bed Holding 1 Another Tight Under The Bloom Moonlight; As The Fan Blow We Shared Warm Kisses Not Knowing My Feelings Will Soon Be Turn 2 Ice, She's In Love With Another Man I Knew Somewhat All My Life, I Treated Her Like A Woman Was Suppose 2 Be Treated, He Was The Opposite From Me He Kept Her Feeling Defeated; Was It Hard 4 Her 2 Recognize I Was A True Friend Indeed, Was It Something I Did And Not Say? Did I Give 2 Much Attention Or Should I Have Given Less Or Is It The Other Way Around? Honesty Was A Lie And If We Could Do It All Over Again I Would Make Her Cry Because Of The Pain I Feel Inside, Now Telling Myself All Women Are The Same Until My Mother And Grandmother Told Me Don't Go After Looks Because Those Are The Ones In The Most Pain, But If U Have A Broken Heart Give It Time And It Will Be Healed Again.
What Happen 2 All That
Love I Gave? What Happen
2 All That Love We Made?
I Hate I Let U In My ♥

DANGEROUS FUN

What Started Out A Game Became Serious It Was Only Supposed 2 Be Fun 4 Awhile But She Had Such An Amazing Smile That Would Drive Any Soul Wild; With Our Desires Similar Should I Challenge This Woman Who Is Looking At Me Like I'm Dinner; Does She Feel Like I Or Does She Fret When We Connect With Our Eyes, I Wish I Could Know But By The Way She's Playing Makes Me Feel Somewhere There's A Guy; Although It Seems We're Both Attracted Should We Be Letting This Happen? Attention Desperately Needed, Security, Confidence, Love Is What She Has Been Deprived Why? Because Her Man Beats Her Cheats And Lies; I Don't Want 2 Be Unfair But Could There Be A Chance 4 Me And U? We Made Love A Few Times But Then We Were Through.

THE ROSE AND HEART

My Heart Is Connected 2 A Rose So If The Rose Die Then Surely So Will I; Our Friendship And True Love 4 Each Other Keeps Us Alive; Profound And Intimate But Fragile 2 The Breath Of Life, The Good Thing Is Our External And Internal Shows A Constant Will 2 Fight Because That Is Our Creed; We Depend On 1 Another So Out Of Love We Emulate 1 Another, We Share Our Equilibrium Stem Rooted 2 Petal Heart Inside The Chest So That Makes Us More Then A Clique. A Gift Of God So We Continue 2 Rise From Crevasse Not Allowing Our Mind And Root 2 Be Barren, Long As Me The Heart Keeps The Rose Her In Beautiful Crescendo Mode I Shall Continue 2 Grow, If Not It Could Become Critical 2 What We Share Edible 4 Those Who Wish 2 Cause Us Nightmares; Love And Life Is What We Provide And If One Of Those Is Taken Away Then That Means We Both Die.

1 ANOTHERS HEART

Last Night All I Could Think 😕 About Was How 2 People Hurt 1 Another Not Even Trying 2, How Could Our Relationship In The Beginning Be So Loving 😊 I Die 4 U U Live 4 Me, 2 Become I Need Some Space Some Time 2 Think 💭 , I Don't Care We're Done; It Was Laughter And Sharing Smiles In The Late Night But Now It's Just Anger And Shedding Tears 😭 In The Day Light; Grown Together 2 Only Grow Apart I Could Just Hope Our Prayers 🙏 Are The Same That We Will Always Have 1 Anothers Heart

2 U I SAY GOODBYE 👋

I'm In Love 😊 With U But I'm Not In Love With Ure Stupidity Repeating The Same Cycle Of Destroying Our Unity; Our Souls Was Once Intertwine Locked 🔒 And Married But Now Because Of Foolish Behavior There Is Nothing But Distance Between Us; I Don't Like The New U I Want The Old U Who I Was Once Compelled By, Being Without U Reminiscing Makes Me Angry 😡 Inside Sometimes Sad 😔 Because At One Point U Were 1 Of The Most Beautiful 🤩 Caring Women I Have Ever Had, But Now I Say Goodbye 👋 4 Good And Will Just Continue 2 Cherish The Love 🩶 We Use 2 Share And Have.

A REAL WOMEN-DEDICATED 2 REAL WOMEN ALL OVER THE 🌍

A Real Women Loves When U See Beyond Her Fleshly Beauty, Knows Her Favorite Color, Pay Attention 2 Small Detail In Conversation And Surprisingly Repeat 🔁 It Back 2 Them In The Long Run; A Real Women Loves When U Carry Her True Feelings Within U, Allow Her 2 Be Free As The Open Seas, And Be The Man 2 Become The Rain 🌧 2 Wash 💨 Away Their Pain; From The Bottom Of Ones Heart 💜 2 The Depth Of Ones Soul U Must Treat A Women As If They Were The Blood 💧 In Ure Veins Straight Shining Diamond 🔷 Fresh Off The African Lands; U Make A Women Whole When U Listen 👂 2 Her Speak 🗣 Her Soul, Show Passion, Give Understanding And When U Know How 2 Bring Forth Rebirth Of Love 💞; U Have 2 Place A Women Into Ure Plans, Make It Ure Business 2 Wipe Away Tears 😭, Knock Down Walls Of Fear And Always Remain 2 Be The 1 They Always Knew; The Lord Knows A Women Hates When U Toy With Her Affection, Have Childish Petty Ways But Loves When U Admit When U Make A Mistake; A Real Women Loves When U Leave Them With No Regrets, Leave A Precious Mark So Deep It's Hard 2 Remove, Be A True Reflection Of Her When Sharing Company And When U Keep Her As A Close Friend Anytime Anywhere; When A Real Women Has Transformed Ure Negativity Into Love 💜 And Life U Must Treat Her As If It Was The Day She Vows 2 Respect U And Be Honest As Ure Wife

BROKEN BUT FREE

Show Me How Deep Love Could Be Or Do U Want 2 Take My Heart Away? Somebody Already Broke My Heart, I've Been Torn Apart So Many Times I Don't Want 2 Play; I Can't Go There Again Cause Love Is Never As Good As The First Time; What Do U Want From Me? What Do U Need From Me? Because If It's Love I Don't Have It Anymore, Understand That My Feelings Are Sore And Know That Pain Is Something I Now Adore; If It's Only My Body, Heart, And Soul That U Wish 2 Seek Then Make A Wish On A ☆ And If It's Meant 2 Be Then It Will Be A We, Until Then It's Only Me So Broken But Free.

BRIGHTER DAY BETTER TOMORROW

I Need A Women Arm 2 Hold Me Because These Nights Are Unkind; Life Is Cruel Painful 😖 And Suffering Without A Women Next 2 Me; In Silence Tears 😨 Fall Like Rain Drops 💧 Inside My Mind Without Appearing From My 👀,My Pain Needs 2 Be Kissed Away So I Could See A Brighter Day Better Tomorrow.

CANDLE LOVE

2 Me At Times Love Could Be Like A Candle Once U Light It It Could Burn 🕯 Out Fast Or Slow; But It Could Last Somewhat Long If U Continue 2 Brake Up 2 Make Up; Light It Then Put It Out, Light It Then Put It Out But Eventually It Still Melts Away Burn 🕯 Out.

FREAK 2 FREAK

Everything Inside Of Me Is Calling And Wanting U, Is It Possible That I've Found Love Deeper As The River Runs? Warmer Then The Morning , So Fly And Unique With A Tasty Smile; If U Were A Fruit U Would Be A Something A Man Like I Just Love 2 Eat, Black And Beautiful Dark And Sweet All I Need 4 U Is 2 Rub My Back And When U Get Off Work From A Hard Day I'll Rub Ure Feet ; U Are The Baby Because U Keep Me Coming Back 4 More, My Bonnie Ure Clyde My Queen Ure King Even Our Souls Collide And ' Wrestle Inside; I Love When She Feels My Vibes From Just Looking In My Eyes; I Don't Know Much About Love But The Little Bit I Do Know I Got It From U, From The Sex 2 The Conversations We Shoot; She Shows Me She Values My Advise And Help, Could I Be Her Greatest Blessing Through Sickness And Health? Likes 2 Make Love All Night Until Both Of Our Strength Is Gone, But My Thing Is Pleasing U Shawty It Makes Me Feel Good Hearing U Scream And Moan From Freak 2 Freak

HOLD ME

I Want 2 Be Held With Open Arms,With Love,With Locked Eyes; I Want 2 Be Held With Words, Hold Me With Real True Comfort From The Bottom Of Ure Heart; Hold Me When I Struggle, Hold Me When I Cry, Hold Me When I've Done Wrong But Show Me In So Many Ways How 2 Live On; Hold My Head Close 2 Ure Heart Beat When Ure Windowpane Is Not Easy, Hold Me 4 When I Show U The Best And Most Grateful Thing In Life Which Is God And Love; Please Just Hold Me , Will U Just Hold Me? U Know All My Faults My Rights My Wrongs, I Just Want 2 Be Held 4ever Long.

YOUNG MOTHERS

Although She Gets Straight A's And B's She Feels Her Life Carry Such Little Worth Until In Her Younger Years When She Gave Child Birth; Baby Father's A Grown Male But A Juvenile Straight Up Adolescent In The Mind Who Knows Nothing About Being A Real Father Sharing Jewels, But He Negates Her Love By Telling Lies; As Her New Born Emerged Into This Broken World Her Child Gave Her A Sense That A Broken Heart Could Be Fixed, But In The Small Corner Of Her Mind She Wishes She Had Someone Special 2 Identify Her Pain With; Daily In Her Existence She's Witnessing Evil ,Her True Dreams Seems Falsified By Life, Her True Sense 4 Her Child Keeps Her From Poisoning Her Own Life; One Thing She Doesn't Know When She Looks Her Baby In The Eyes He/She Knows What She Feels Inside Then Her Rose Smile And Laugh No Longer Does She Feel Completely Empty Inside Although Her Baby Daddy's Not Around 2 Guide; She's Enjoying The Scenery As She's Becoming A Diamond Watching Her Diamond Sparkle In The Midsts Of The Mire.
I Understand U,And I
Love U When U Think
Nobody Else Does Young
Mothers.

WOMAN

I Like 2 See A Woman Shed Tears Because It Shows So Many Beautiful And Precious Expressions Especially When Innocent, It's Easy 2 Capture Their Hearts If Treated Right; Open Minded And Could Be Vulnerable Just Like Kids, They're Sensitive; I Love When She Knows She's A Queen, Their Voices Are So Soft And Sweet U Could Tell That They're Real Woman By The Way They Speak; Although Most Of Them Raised Themselves Where Do They Find The Power 2 Love Someone Else? Their Mind, Heart, And Body Go Through So Many Changes When Going Through Ministration U Could See It In Their Faces; When Mistreated They Feel At Times So Defeated Lost And Incomplete; Although I Am A Man I Have A Mother And Plenty Of Sisters So I Understand; My Heart Goes Out 2 Every Woman And Girl Who's Trying 2 Make It In This Hard And Cruel World; God Bless Any New Born Girl That They Bloom Into A Woman And Become The Flower Of Someones Garden.

WHY DONT U LIKE HER

Why Dont U Like Her Is It Because She Has Chose 2 Step Out Into The World 🌑 And Spread Her Wings And Soar Through The Clouds ☁?Why Dont U Like Her Is It Because She Moves Without Fear, Accomplishes Her Dreams While Not Being Afraid 😨 2 Do Or Say What She Feels? Why Dont U Like Her Is It Because She Feels She's Not 2 Thick Or Skinny, She's Just Right From Her Head 2 Her Feet 🦶,Walks With Grace In Her Hips, Has Nice Sexy Lips 👄, Hair Is Not A Weave Nor 2 Short But Is Nicely Placed Upon Her Shoulders, Carrying A Different Type Of Beauty Because She Posses A Strong 💪 Confidence? Why Dont U Like Her Is It Because When She Speak 🗣 She Is Eloquent, Dress With Elegance That Makes People Gravitate Towards Her? Why Dont U Like Her When She Shows U Love 💜, Empower U, Fight 4 U, Teaches U How 2 Love And Become A Better U 4 U? Why Dont U Like Her When She Shows U She's Not Perfect And Makes Mistakes, And Rain 🌧 Does Comes Her Way? Why Dont U Like This Women Is It Because U Wish U Were Her?

WHAT LOVE MEANS

Don't Treat Me Bad Because Who I Am Pay Attention 2 My Truest Thoughts Truest Feelings, 4 Get The Dope Guns And Old Girlfriends That Use 2 Have Me Sprung; I'm Not Trying 2 Burden U Or Have U Hurting I'm Changing So U Don't Have 2 Worry About Me Doing 2 Much Flirting, 2 Me U're My Ghetto Virgin So That Gives My Wild Heart A New Purpose, My Love Is Unconditional And Unforgettable Always Spiritual; It's Hard Being Who I Am And U Got My Heart So Take It Into Consideration I'm Not Other Men, Be My Friend Always And U Will See Who I Really Am; Share My Dream And I'll Show U 2 Me What Love Feels Like And Mean.

WE DON'T EXIST ANYMORE

U Almost 😁 Turned Me Into My Own Worse Enemy When It Came 2 U Somehow; I Wasn't Free Because I Was Bound 2 U, When I Use 2 Look 👀 Into Ure Light Brown Eyes I Seen A Passion U Had 4 Me I Never Knew What Was Happening Between Us Was Magic, But 2 Many Mistakes Caused By Us Both Is What Made Our Hearts Break; We Use 2 Pull Back One Another Hand ✋ 2 Stay But Now We Don't Exist Anymore, From Each Other We Have Faded Away.

TRUTH

I Taught Myself Not 2 Disillusion No 1 I'm Close 2 Too Always Maintain Truth Because Honesty Is A Beauty, It's Like A Pleasant Smell 👃 2 Me Something I'm Attracted 2; Why Does It Seem Like The Woman I'm Involved With Wants 2 Be Lied 🙁 2? Is It Because Hazy Vision Is What She's Use 2? Right Now I Feel Desolate, Angry 😠 And Confused 👻 Because I Was Being Sincere About What's Going On In My Life And Her Reply Was A Rude Attitude; I Hope She Wasn't Just Some Brief Romantic That Sold Me A Dream Cause I Told The Truth.

POETIC TRUTH

U Say U Miss Me But Inside Ure Head I'm Barely 😧 Ever Thought 💭 About; U Say U Love Me But U Allow So Many Others Ure Love Outside Of Me; U Said That U Care And Shall Wait 4 Me, Instead U Walked Away Without Showing Any Concern; Now That I'm About 2 Get Out U Said I Can't Wait Until U Come Home 🏠 And I Smiled And Said Fuck U Cause When I Was Doing Bad U I Couldn't Call 📞, I Hope 🤞 U Had Fun Because I've Moved On.
Don't Look At Me Like
I Did Something Wrong 😑
Because I Kept It Real
In This Poem

HOLD ME

I Want 2 Be Held With Open Arms,With Love,With Locked Eyes; I Want 2 Be Held With Words, Hold Me With Real True Comfort From The Bottom Of Ure Heart; Hold Me When I Struggle, Hold Me When I Cry, Hold Me When I've Done Wrong But Show Me In So Many Ways How 2 Live On; Hold My Head Close 2 Ure Heart Beat When Ure Windowpane Is Not Easy, Hold Me 4 When I Show U The Best And Most Grateful Thing In Life Which Is God And Love; Please Just Hold Me , Will U Just Hold Me? U Know All My Faults My Rights My Wrongs, I Just Want 2 Be Held 4ever Long.

I CARE

Are U Not Happy? Then Come My Child And Let Me Give U Smile 😊 4 I Am Here When U Cry No Matter Boy/Girl 2 Dry Ure 👀, And When U Hurt 😔 Let Me Take Some Of The Pain And Release What Makes U Feel Shame; With Hearts 🖤 Full Of Gold I Wish U Luck 2 Be In The Warmest Position Instead Of The Cold 😬; I Am 2 Take Away All Of Ure Fears And Bring U A Smile 4 Another Year!! I Hope 🙏 And Pray 4 Better Days That The Sun 🌼 Shine In All Of Ure Ways; Right Now Day's Are Short But Nights Are Long Call ☎ 2 Me If In Need Of Help And I'll Guide Ure Hearts 🤍 Where It Belongs, So Hold On At The Same Time Be Strong 💪 I'm With U Until Thee End 4 Ever My Love Will Be Shown So Know That I Care If Nobody Else Cares.

4 The Hearts 🖤
That Need Love
Yo Soul Is My Soul
Yo Pain Is My Pain
My Care Is Ure Care
4 Ever Fair When No
Ones 👆 There
I Care If Don't Nobody
Else Care

I FELT HOW I FELT IN SECRECY

In Secrecy My Feelings Begin 2 Grow 4 U And I Did Not Say A Word Because I Had No Idea 👻 Of Ure Perception Of Me Or Thought 💭 U Wouldn't Have Understood Me; Ure Long Curly Jet Black Hair And Thick Eyebrows Brought Out Ure Dimples Even More When U Decided 2 Show That Beautiful Smile 😊; U Were My Dream That I Wanted 2 Turn Into My Reality But In The amidst Of My Young Life I Was Troublesome And Full Of Chaos, 2 Many Of My Mistakes Caused Us 2 Separate 2 Soon; Sometimes I Glance At The Pictures In My Head Of U And Wonder 💭 Why At The Most Awkward Time I Wanted 2 Express My Truth How I Felt 4 U, And That's When U Wrapped Embraced Ure Jesus Chain Around My Neck And Kissed Me On My Lips 2 Say Goodbye 👋 And That's When I Knew U Felt How I Felt; I Swear I Wish I Knew Where U Were, If U're Alright, Or Needed Any Type Of Help Because Of What We Both Felt Will No Longer Have 2 Be In Secrecy.

PROUD OF U

I'm Proud Of U Because Of The Trials And Tribulations I've Seen U Overcome; I'm Proud Of U Because U Respect Ure Gift That God Has Blessed U With 2 Carry On; I'm Proud Of U Because U Never Gambled With Ure Integrity, Allowed Just Anyone An Invitation Into Ure Interior; Ure Photos Are Quality So That Makes U Quality, They Are What U Intended Them 2 Be Poetic Deep So I'm Proud Of U; This Photo Wasn't Disregarded Because When I Glanced At It I Knew It Measure 📏 Up 2 What U Wanted It 2 Be So That's What Made Me Proud Of U 👍; I Know Ure Precious Daughter Is Proud Of U And Ure Family 2, Proud Of U 👍 Is What I Am But Be More Proud Of Yourself Because It's U Who Is The Star ⭐ The Diamond 💎 That Is Making U Shine; Keep Sparkling ✨ And Being Proud Gods On Black Ebony Child.

LOVE

Let's Not Waste Our Time Arguing And Fighting Let's Be 2 Busy Being In Love Me And U Because Yes I Love U With All My Heart And Soul; This Is How I Feel Right Now And Want 2 Feel It 4 Ever More, Oh Lord Boo A.K.A Shorty I Need Ure Soul And U Could Have Mines All U Have 2 Do Is Grab Hold And Don't Let Go This Is The Joy We Both Need; Let Me Be Ure Dream Come True 2 Life, Ure Moon, Sun, And Starlight; I'm The Candle U're The Fire We Belong Together Let's Melt One Another's Passion No Talk Just All Lights Camera Action Starring U Called Beautiful U; Look What Love Made Me Do, Although I Was Raised In The Ghetto My Mother Told Me 2 Keep My Love True One Love One Heart One Soul It's All 4 U Why Do I Feel This Way?
Why Have I Even Spoken This Way? Why? Do I Still Believe In Love

U AND ME

Before Our Paths Has Crossed We Must Have Met In The Spiritual World Somewhere, Although I Rarely Say A Word 2 U I Rather Let My Verbs Be A Thousand Words; What I Feel 4 U Is Complex Truly Difficult, I Want 2 Connect Our Body, Mind, And Spirit All The Way; Underneath My Flesh Is A Million Different Vibes I Wish 2 Lay Upon Ure Heart Sensations Never Felt Before, This Passionate Feeling Will 4 Sure Be Appealing Intimate Always If U Want From Day 2 Night, Quiet Conversations Letting Our Eyes Do The Talking Will Start A Gentle Spark; I'm With The Fun Love Mind Games So Let Ure Mind Embrace Them, If U're Willing Like I'm Willing And Feeling Like I'm Feeling U Be The Icing And I'll Be The Cake Let's Come Together And Be A Bomb Taste Just U And Me.

LOVE

Who Ever Said That Love Was Easy 2 Find They Must Be Out Their Damn Rabbit Minds; At Times Love Is Never Completely Understood,Sometimes Love Could Be Like Kind Words But It Comes And Goes; Day After Day Seems Like I Put All My Dreams Aside 4 Love, At About 20yrs Young I Began 2 Wake Up Down On My Luck Looking 4 Love; In My Life It's Like Love Don't Belong, I Thought Lust Was Love And I Hate What Lust Has Done 2 Me But I Hate What I Have Done 2 Myself 4 Love; I Believe And See Now Love Is More Then Words It's An Expression, It's Beautiful, Precious, And A Pure Song; I Use 2 Feel Like It Was Love That Brings U Down And Treat U Wrong Make U Feel Like U Don't Belong ,Kill Softly Brake And Destroys Homes; I Use 2 Think Love Made Me Feel So Alone How Would I Find The Strength 2 Continue On Without A Little Bit Of Love,But 2 Be Honest Love Has No Right Or Wrong It's Just Something We All Have 2 Embrace Good Or Bad; I Guess Love Is Something We All Need And Must Have Because With It U Feel Very Much Alive And Without It U're Mentally,Soulfully Crushed And That's Just Love 4 That Ass.
It Was Lust Not Love
That Has Blinded Me,
What I Use Be Im Not Anymore

JUST U I'M AFTER

It's Raining Outside And The Wind Is Blowing Tough Watching Movies On A Small Ghetto T.V That U Turn With A Fork; Sitting Next 2 Me On The Couch Is This Precious Soul Who Looks So Good I Call My Women, Come Closer So I Could Hold U In My Arms, Kiss U, Keep Each Other Warm; Speaking Softly In My Ear All Up In My Head I Believe In U With Faith, Then I Whispered We Were Meant 4 One Another That's Why We're Here On This Earth; We Both Feel Humility With Grace, My Nature Is Growing Up Her Womb Is On 🐣 4 Pleasure With Desire, Extremely Enjoying My Tongues Pleasure Her Body Has An Bomb Taste, Going With The Flow She Looks Me In The 👀 With A Smile Of U Could Have It Ure Way; Her 👀 Begin 2 Close Slow Our Affection Intensified More And More, As She Let Me Inside Her Body Magic Begin And Brought Forth A Glow; Caressing Her Hair With My Hand Saying Don't Let Me Go If Only 4 A Moment Give Me Hope, Although We Made It Through Plenty Fights With Laughter Ure Body, Mind, And 👀, Thoughts, Soul, 🤍 And Voice Is All I'm After.

LOVE IS LOVELY

Making Love With My Heart Keeps The Passion Sweet, Kissing While Licking Certain Parts Of The Face And Body Makes Me Become More Of A Freak; When I Touch Certain Spots U Moan That Makes Me Continue On With Pleasure, I'm More Dangerous When I'm Between Those Inner Thighs Making U 😬 With My 👅 Moving Awkward Towards Ure Middle Like A 🐍; Look In My 👀 Feel My 🔥,What At This Point Is Ure Desire? What Is Ure Fantasy? Don't Turn Ure 👀 From Mines Do Not Release Ure Juices Just Yet Hold It Until U Lose Control Of Yourself And Just Forget About Everybody Who Hated U Or Made U Sick; Turn Over Shhhh Don't Say A Word As I Lick Down Ure Back Touching Every Single Curb, I Struck A Nerve That Makes The Spine Curve; Will U Love Me In The Morning 4 Eternity? Because Love Is Lovely.

STRONG ALTHOUGH LONELY

Am I Wrong 4 Wanting 2 Love Selfishly 2 Keep Someone Heart And Cherish It Like My Own Although I Played The Hard Role On So Many If They Would Have Punched Me They Would Have Seen That I Have Feelings And Bleed; Mixing Honesty With Lies I Use 2 Be The One Laughing Now I'm The One Crying 😢, I Was Told Misery Loves Company Now I See Why; Hustling Brought Money 💵 With Weman Which Turned Me Into A Snake 🐍 With Fangs And Venom, So Many Said They No Longer Want 2 Be With Me But When I Turn 2 Go Away They Pull Back My Hand ✋ 2 Stay; Play Fighting With Make Up Sex Going Deep Inside Their Bodies Brought An Ecstasy Upon Them As Well As Me,Some I Loved Some I Did Not Some Were Cute Some Where Not And Now That I'm Alone I Remember Every Single Soul That I Made Heart 🖤 Drop, Now That I'm Older I Rather Rap, Smoke Blunts But Stay Away From Croocked Schemes And Plots But If Love Comes Back Around I'll Make Sure Our Relationship Stays Hot Sincerely Raymond

I Feel Strong Although I'm Lonely 😪

MY EYES 👀

Some Say When They Look Into My Eyes 👀 They See So Many Hopes And Wishes, One Who Could Bring Some Back 2 Redemption Who Could Kindle Flames 🔥 Intoxicate A Mind Without Using A Drug Substance; They Say They Could See My Pure Beating Heart 💜 Through My Eyes, If They Could See All This Through My Eyes Then Why Don't They Understand The Tears 😭 I Cry 🙁? The Profound 🙂 Pain I Constantly Feel Inside? Could They See I Use 2 Be Blind Now One Day I Shall Rise In My Eyes 👀.

THERE ARE SO MANY

There Are So Many Broken 😔 Hearts That Just Wish That Were Unbroken, So Many Tears 😨 That Has Fallen From Hurtful Eyes That Wish 2 Be Wiped Away By A Pleasant Hand ✋ That Only Care 4 And Love Them; So Many Lives Has Been Left In The Rain ☁️ ☂️ That Wish They Had Someone With Warm Arms 2 Release Them From Pain; There Are So Many Who Wish That When They Heard Their Partner Say They Love Them It Will Always Remain The Same And Never Change; There Are So Many Who Wish That They Had Someone 2 Make Them Forget About Their Past Who Open Their Heart 🖤 2 A Whole New Style, Who Wish They Had Someone 2 Place Ease On Their Mind 2 Leave Bad Memories Behind.

BRIGHTER DAY BETTER TOMORROW

I Need A Women Arm 2 Hold Me Because These Nights Are Unkind;

WE DON'T EXIST ANYMORE

U Almost 😄 Turned Me Into My Own Worse Enemy When It Came 2 U Somehow; I Wasn't Free Because I Was Bound 2 U, When I Use 2 Look 👀 Into Ure Light Brown Eyes I Seen A Passion U Had 4 Me I Never Knew What Was Happening Between Us Was Magic, But 2 Many Mistakes Caused By Us Both Is What Made Our Hearts Break; We Use 2 Pull Back One Another Hand ✋ 2 Stay But Now We Don't Exist Anymore, From Each Other We Have Faded Away

WHY DONT U LIKE HER

Why Dont U Like Her Is It Because She Has Chose 2 Step Out Into The World And Spread Her Wings And Soar Through The Clouds ?Why Dont U Like Her Is It Because She Moves Without Fear, Accomplishes Her Dreams While Not Being Afraid 2 Do Or Say What She Feels? Why Dont U Like Her Is It Because She Feels She's Not 2 Thick Or Skinny, She's Just Right From Her Head 2 Her Feet ,Walks With Grace In Her Hips, Has Nice Sexy Lips , Hair Is Not A Weave Nor 2 Short But Is Nicely Placed Upon Her Shoulders, Carrying A Different Type Of Beauty Because She Posses A Strong Confidence? Why Dont U Like Her Is It Because When She Speak She Is Eloquent, Dress With Elegance That Makes People Gravitate Towards Her? Why Dont U Like Her When She Shows U Love , Empower U, Fight 4 U, Teaches U How 2 Love And Become A Better U 4 U? Why Dont U Like Her When She Shows U She's Not Perfect And Makes Mistakes, And Rain Does Comes Her Way? Why Dont U Like This Women Is It Because U Wish U Were Her?

TRUTH

I Taught Myself Not 2 Disillusion No 1 I'm Close 2 Too Always Maintain Truth Because Honesty Is A Beauty, It's Like A Pleasant Smell 👃 2 Me Something I'm Attracted 2; Why Does It Seem Like The Woman I'm Involved With Wants 2 Be Lied 🙁 2? Is It Because Hazy Vision Is What She's Use 2? Right Now I Feel Desolate, Angry 😠 And Confused 👻 Because I Was Being Sincere About What's Going On In My Life And Her Reply Was A Rude Attitude; I Hope She Wasn't Just Some Brief Romantic That Sold Me A Dream Cause I Told The Truth.

WE SHARE LAUGHTER

4 Some Reason Our Paths Crossed Again But I Chose Only 2 Be Friends Because Of My Lifestyle That Could Hurt 😔 U As Once Before, But Yet Everything About U Is Becoming So Much Harder 2 Ignore; When We Speak 🧑 And Share Hearts 😄 There's No Pretending Or Myths Only Revealing Of Our True Traits We Are Injecting Into One Another's Mind Frame; Because She Is So Down And True I Allow Her 2 Diss Miss Me Quickly Cause Of What I Put Her Through, Beautiful Always 😺 And Bravery Is What She Has Added 2 Her Character; I Relate 2 Her In More Of A Major Way Now Because She Has Become More Like 👍 Me And Understanding My Character, Back Then My Fast 🖐 Living Didn't Allow Us 2 Share Laughter But Now We Notice Each Other More And Share A Pure Laughter.

I Enjoy 😊 Ure Smile 😊 It Provides Peace ✌

IN LOVE 😁 SINGLE

I'm Single But In Love 🤩 With A Soul Who Share My Common Characteristics, We Quote, Mimic, And Represent 1 Another As Friends Do; We Share A Genuine Magnetism Because 4 Some Reason Our Pain And Misery Celebrates 🎆 Together; We Go Together Like Creativity With The Vision, Music And Rhythm 🎶, Lyrics With A Bomb 💣 Beat; Her Terminology Keeps Me Gone Out My Mind Clutching My Heart 💜, I Guess It's The Way She Pierce Me With Her Soothing Influential Appropriate Speech 🗡; I Can't Deny Although I'm Single My Heart 💜 Is Not Vacant, Her Whole Beauty Is Rich And It Floods Me Has Me Captivated 🤩, But I Must Remain This Way Until My Ways Are No Longer Inappropriate Till I Recognize I'm Trust Worthy As A Romantic Partner; But U Know One Thing About Being In Love 😁 Single Although The Feelings Are Strong 💪 It Doesn't Cause Disaster Promote Chaos It Actually Keeps Us Close Like Animals That Live Together On The Mountain ⛰ Tops.

2 U I SAY GOODBYE 👋

I'm In Love 😊 With U But I'm Not In Love With Ure Stupidity Repeating The Same Cycle Of Destroying Our Unity; Our Souls Was Once Intertwine Locked 🔒 And Married But Now Because Of Foolish Behavior There Is Nothing But Distance Between Is; I Don't Like The New U I Want The Old U Who I Was Once Compelled By, Being Without U Reminiscing Makes Me Angry 😠 Inside Sometimes Sad 😔 Because At One Point U Were 1 Of The Most Beautiful 🤩 Caring Women I Have Ever Had, But Now I Say Goodbye 👋 4 Good And Will Just Continue 2 Cherish The Love 💝 We Use 2 Share And Have.

MINES IN DO TIME

U Use 2 Be Hard 2 Define, Clarify, A Proud ⬜ Fine Women Who Made Me Feel A Sensation I Could Not Describe; Before We Have Ever Even Spoken Ure Beauty Had Stalked My Mind Like The Shadows
On The Wall; Rocking Open Toe High Hills With Classy School Teacher 🧑 Type Of Outfits And French Tips U Would Come Through And Shut It Down Where Ever I May Sit; I'm Old Enough 2 Understand That Love 🤍 Could Hurt ☹ So Bad But I Also Know That It Could Feel So Good, And There's Something About U That Made Me Willing 2 Take The Risk And I Had 2 Show U That My Intentions Was Good; Anticipation Wouldn't Allow Me 2 Shake The Feeling What I Wanted U 2 Know, The Move That I Bust Was Smooth So It Allowed My Thoughts 💭 2 Flow; As Months Sailed On By U Were No Longer Shy 🙈 And I Left U With Loving 😌 Words That U Shall Hang On 2 For Ever Because Ure Heart 🤍 Burn 🔥 From The Words I Spoke; I Remember U Saying I Want 2 Learn What U Want 2 Teach Me, So I Begin 2 Run My Fingers Down Ure Spine, U Begin 2 Shiver And I Could Read The Freaky Things On Ure Mind, Ure Knees Became Weak While My Kisses 😚 Made U Dizzy 😵 In The Head; U Pulled Me Into Ure Personal Private Space And Made Yourself Mines.

LONG AWAITED LOVER

U Are Innocence Straight Essence At Its Purest Form I Was Just A Body With Flesh Covered Over It With A Diamond 💎 Spirit, My Smile 😀 Was So Very Seldom Which Made Which Made U So Very Curious 🙂; Sworn 2 Secrecy 2 A Facade Appearance But In The Cut Of My Thoughts 💭 It Was Evident That U Would Unveil And Draw Information From My Tortured Soul Possibly Be The Remedy 2 Heal It; Ure Academics On Love 💜 Was Gentle Which Made Me Gravitate Towards U But It Was Hard 2 Love U 🐱 When Another Part Of My Nature Died Inside Of Me; Before Me Essential Ferlings Of Mines Begin 2 Lose Its Value Afraid 😱 2 Be Shown But U Pursued Me In The Way That A Man Would Do A Women When She Is Scorn; Just When I Was Being Chocked And About 2 Wither Away From Life Pouring Rain 🌧 U Arrived Like The Sun 🌞 God Hand ✋ 2 Relieve My Pain And 4 That 2 Me Tranquillity Should Be Ure Name; Now I Work Hard 2 Find The Perfect 🎶 Lyrics 2 Assist Me In This Complex Matter That Really Should Be Simplistic When I Speak 🗣 2 This Long Awaited Lover Who's Patiently Standing Right Before Me.

WEAK

Sometimes Being Strong 💪 Could Make U Weak Brake U Down, Make U Feel Low 2 Where U Feel Like What Else Is There 2 Live 4, So We Sing Spiritual Songs Of Old 2 Lead Us Down The Long And Rough Road; Strength Is Starting 2 Lose Its Grip Like An Old Man Or Women Who Has Blown Out A Hip Or Been Broken 😞 Down By A Slave Master From His Whip; Sometimes U Could Feel So Weak U Become Speechless 😶 As If U Were Force 2 Submit 2 Defeat, Heart Does Nothing But Sleep 😴 Like A Prisoner Because Doesn't Want 2 Feel The Pain, And All This Comes Along When Ure Subject 2 Change Or Being In The Game, Or Even A Family Man, And Just Being A Black Man; Sometimes U Could Feel So Weak That Ure Prayers 🙏 No Longer Prayers 🙏 They Become A Weak Man Or Women Who No Longer Has Anything 2 Give Or Share, But When It Get 2 That Point Lift Up Ure Voice Loud As U Can Put Ure Right Hand ✋ Up And Talk 2 God; No Longer Will U Be A Weak Women Or Man, The Lord He Bends And Shapes Us Because It's His Plan 2 Show Us We Really Only Have 1 True Father And Friend.

MY DIARY 📖 DEDICATED 2 MY DIARY

U Are Where I Place My Dreams 💭 And Thoughts Into My Reality Steps Into View; U Are Who I Express My Ghetto Passion 2, U're My Relief 😄, My Rhythm 🎵 Of Life, The Diary 📖 I Place My Rhymes And Beautiful Healed And Unhealed Scars; U Seen When My Smiles 😃 Turned Into Tears 😭 And When My Tears 😭 Turned Into Smiles 😊; U Hold My Writing ✍ Marks Of Beauty, Compassion, Kindness, Wonderful Passions, And Purity But Also Lonely 😔 Nights When Jail And Life Became Hard; Ure Tender Heart 🤍 Is What I Scribe My Rare Beauty On So That Makes U My Fountain Of Love 🖤, My Eyes 👀 And Hands 🙌 Can Not Resist Reading The Conceived Thoughts 💭 Upon Ure Breast; Every Type Of Category, Performance Is Placed Into U, I Pursue U 2 Place My Academic Freedom And U Participated Without Saying A Word; U Have Always Revived Me Without Making Me Feel Foreign Inside, U Don't Try 2 Hold My Identity In Captivity; This Is My Voice On Ure Tongue 😛 U Are The One That Will Make Sure Everybody Remember Me, 2 My Diary 📖.

JUST POETRY FROM MY HEART ♡

Many Nights And Hours I Laid Upon A Cot Staring At The Ceiling Letting My Imagination 💭 Run Wild Especially After I've Read Autobiographies And Real Literature That Speaks 👤 My Lifestyle; After I Read Honest Philosophy I Felt Close 2 The Dead Their True Unfailing Love And Honest Values Through Expression They've Shared, It's Always Then Alone In Darkness I Will Begin 2 Cry 😭 Because Screaming Inside Of Me Is Their Souls Their Testimonies And Their Dreams 🛏 Are Now Mines; Through Me These Ghost 👻 Channel Their Anger Constructively Without Deception Although Locked 🔒 In This Cell, Castle Walls, We Concentrate On The Conception That Could Reunite Us But Peace Has 2 Be Our Destination But If Not Hurl Me Into The Next Existence Where Music 🎼 Love And Dancing 💃 Is Forever Existing; So 4 Now This Could Only Be Poetry Written Down From My Heart ♡.

REJECTION

U Could See The Scars Of Pain Written On My Face, I Carry The Cemetery With Me In My Heart ♥ Because That's What's Taking My Hearts Place; I Have Shown Love 4 Mankind But They Make It So Hard 2 Embrace, 4 Them I'll Be Brave I'll Bend Down 2 A River Of Water ☙ When They're Weak 2 Place Water ◌ Inside My Hands 🤲 2 Bring It 2 Their Lips 2 Give Them A Drink; They Say That Love Gets Better With Time So My Arms Has Always Been Open Without Prejudice Or Charging A Dime, But My Category Separates Me From Them Because I'm Brave With A Sensitive Spirit, I Bare My Own Cross Without Fearing; A Man Who Speaks 🗣 Poetic Justice So The World 🌐 Should Be Able 2 Feel Heart Beat, But Instead Before They Like 👍 Me They Had Judge 👤 Me Even Though I Presented Myself Not Ugly; Inside Of Me Now A War Rages There Are A Lot Of People Willing 2 Make My Life A Living Hell Instead Of Trying 2 Engage In My Personality 2 Help Guide Some 2 Change; Once Was A Friend 2 The World 🌐 Now I Feel Like A Ghost 👻 In The Dark, My Brave But Sensitive Spirit Still Love And Care 4 The Humans That Is In It Even Though Plenty Of Times They Tore Me Apart; I Was Only Trying 2 Help Us Make It 2 Where We Belong But Instead They Exchanged My Help 4 Rejection And Stones.

YOUNG MOTHERS

Although She Gets Straight A's And B's She Feels Her Life Carry Such Little Worth Until In Her Younger Years When She Gave Child 😊 Birth; Baby 😊 Father's A Grown Male But A Juvenile Straight Up Adolescent In The Mind Who Nothing About Being A Real Father Sharing Jewels 🔻, But He Negates Her Love 🤍 By Telling Lies; As Her New Born Emerged Into This Broken 😞 World 🌍 Her Child 👶 Gave Her A Sense That A Broken Heart 💔 Could Be Fixed, But In The Small Corner Of Her Mind She Wishes She Had Someone Special 2 Identify Her Pain With; Daily In Her Existence She's Witnessing Evil 👹,Her True Dreams Seems Falsified By Life, Her True Sense 4 Her Child 😊 Keeps Her From Poisoning Her Own Life; One Thing She Doesn't Know When She Looks Her Baby 😊 In The Eyes 👀 He/She Knows What She Feels Inside Then Her Rose 🌹 Smile 😊 And Laugh 😆 No Longer Does She Feel Completely Empty Inside Although Her Baby Daddy's Not Around 2 Guide; She's Enjoying The Scenery As She's Becoming A Diamond 🔶 Watching Her Diamond 💎 Sparkle ⬜ In The Midsts Of The Mire.
I Understand U,And I
Love U When U Think 💭
Nobody Else Does Young
Mothers

MY OWN HEART

Where Is The Room 4 U In Ure Own Heart? The Feeling Of Security And Comfort? With Pure Reason U Relieve Everyone Else Of Their Fears And Pains That Are Deeply Personal, U Left Them With Unforgettable Memories On Their Hearts No Matter Arguments Or Laughter; When Did U Have Time 2 Console Ure Own Heart When Life Reality Left U With A Puzzled Expression Without Merry? Helping Everyone Else Fight 2 Survive Against Their Odds U Couldn't See That U Were The One Odd, What Was The Reason U Were Unapproachable 2 Ure Own Heart But It Was Easy 4 U 2 Uncover Lifes Truth With Poetic Rhymes In Our Eyes? 2 Me U Are The Most Capable, Qualified, Trustworthy Person I Know Because U Explained In A Mature Way It's Hard 2 Live This Life Without God So We Must Ask 4 Forgiveness; Ure Mindset Was So Complex U Would Never Think That U Were From The Projects, U Made Others Feel Stability When Most Wouldn't Even Care, U Were Fearless, A Genius At Work, A Military Hood Soldier Who Cares; I'll Probably Never Understand Ure Ways But Everyday I Use 2 See U Working Hard Just 2 Change Ure Ways So I Know U Love Yourself, But Where Was The Space 4 U In Ure Own Heart That U May Exhale Relax And Take A Break? I Guess Thrilling Risk And Confrontation Committed 2 The Struggle 4 Life Was The Reason From My Own Heart I Stayed Away.

9 7 9 8 5 7 6 1 8 0 5 5 4